ALFRED's
SACRED PERFORMER

COLLECTIONS

MW00812136

The Best *of* Cindy Berry

10 Solo Piano Arrangements of Her Original Choral Works

Arranged by Cindy Berry

I count it a special blessing and privilege to be able to write down my expressions of worship to the Lord and then have others use those songs in their own times of worship. Through the years, about half of my writing has been for piano and the other half for church choirs. Not long ago, my friends at Alfred invited me to consider a unique concept. They asked me to choose some of my best-selling choral anthems and arrange them for solo piano. *The Best of Cindy Berry* is the result of that invitation. This collection offers many stylistically diverse selections, ranging from the flowing ballad *By the Gentle Waters* to the syncopated *Go Ye!* Also included are *Remember Me* (a communion selection), the soaring *Yours Is the Kingdom*, and *I Give You Praise*. Lyrics are included at the end of the book to enhance your times of worship as you play these arrangements. I pray that God will bless you as you use your unique gifts to praise Him at the piano!

Cindy Berry

Alfred

I Give You Praise

Cindy Berry

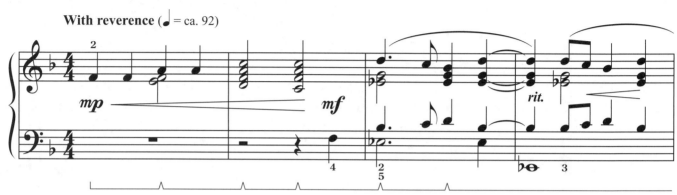

Go Ye!

Cindy Berry

REMEMBER ME

Cindy Berry

(*Approx. Performance Time – 4:00*)

I Will Keep My Eyes on You

Cindy Berry

New Every Morning

Cindy Berry

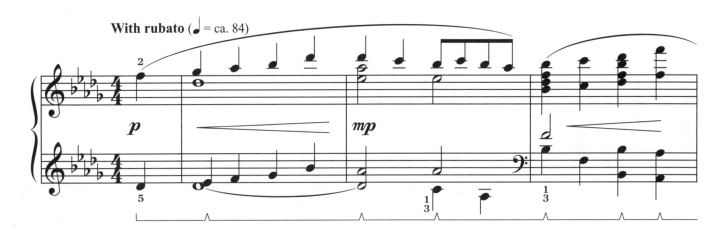

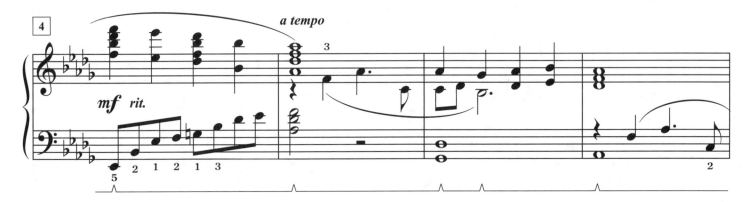

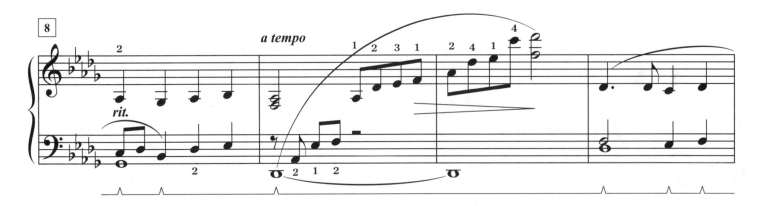

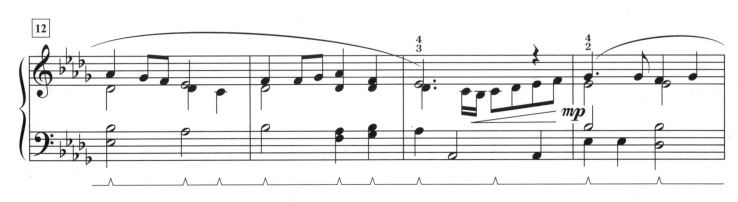

Gentle Waters

Cindy Berry

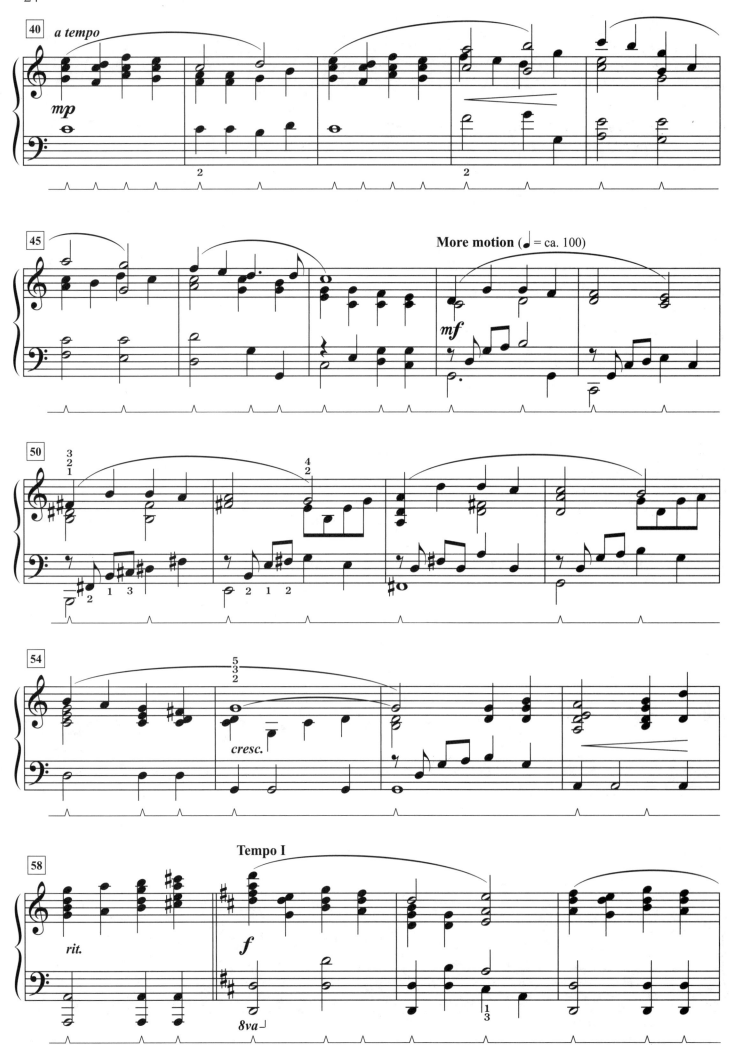

Almighty, Unchangeable God

Cindy Berry

(Approx. Performance Time – 2:45)

Yours Is the Kingdom

Cindy Berry

A Strong Tower

(Approx. Performance Time – 3:00)

Cindy Berry

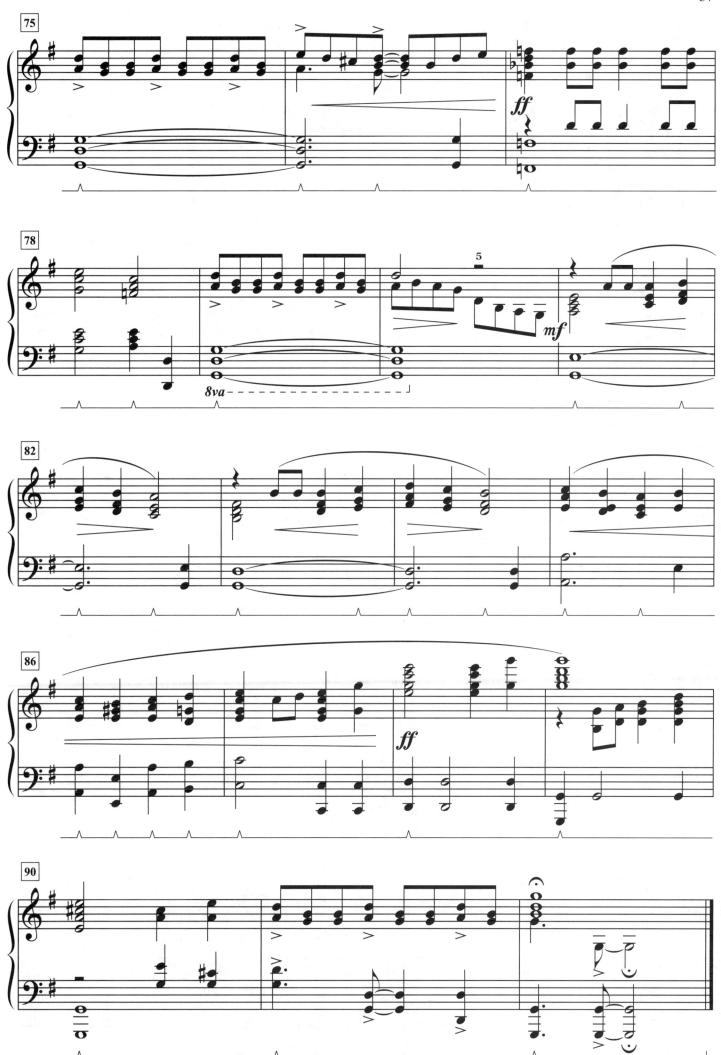

JOY OVERFLOWING

Cindy Berry

With joy (♩. = ca.60)

I GIVE YOU PRAISE

For the splendor of the earth, for the night that turns to day,
For the thunder, loud and glorious, and the lightning's grand display,
For the vastness of the seas, and the mountains, straight and tall,
I praise You, Creator of all.

Refrain:
Praise, I give You praise.
You are mighty King eternal; wondrous are Your ways.
You are holy, holy. I will serve You all my days.
As long as I have breath, I'll give You praise.

For the precious gift of Jesus, who left His heavenly home above,
Offering us salvation, and Your glorious gift of love,
For Your wondrous Holy Spirit bringing comfort, joy and peace,
My song of praise to You will never cease.

Bridge:
And when my life on earth is over, and I stand in You complete,
In reverence I will worship at Your feet.

Words and Music by CINDY BERRY
© 2004 ALFRED PUBLISHING CO., INC.
This Arrangement © 2009 ALFRED PUBLISHING CO., INC.
All Rights Reserved

GO YE!

Refrain:
Go ye into all the world, telling that Jesus lives;
Lifting high the cross, whatever the cost,
Sharing the love He gives.
Go ye into all the world, spreading the Word of Life.
Go and gladly share with people everywhere;
Go in the name of Christ.

We are His hands to show compassion,
We are His feet to spread the message of love.
By sowing gospel seeds, meeting others' needs,
We glorify our Father above.

Bridge:
To spread His love to every land,
To reach out a helping hand,
To do whatever the Lord commands—
That is our desire, our desire.

Words and Music by CINDY BERRY
© 1998 VAN NESS PRESS, INC. (ASCAP)
(Administered by LIFEWAY WORSHIP MUSIC GROUP)
This Arrangement © 2009 VAN NESS PRESS, INC. (ASCAP)
All Rights Reserved including Public Performance   Used by Permission

REMEMBER ME

In the upper room in Jerusalem, Jesus gathered with His friends,
For He knew the day was drawing near when His life on earth would end.
As they met for the Passover meal, they heard their Master pray.
They saw Him take the wine and the bread, and then they heard Him say,

Refrain:
Remember Me, remember Me. Oh, may it ever be.
As you drink the cup and eat the bread,
Remember, remember Me.

It was a special time of fellowship, but soon they would depart.
And the memories of this moment they would cherish in their heart.
But as they ate of this final meal, His disciples could not understand
That Jesus, the only Son of God would become the Passover Lamb.

Bridge:
This is My body, broken for you; Now take and eat this bread.
And this cup is my blood of the covenant. For you My blood is shed.

Words and Music by CINDY BERRY
© 1996 HAL LEONARD CORPORATION
This Arrangement © 2009 HAL LEONARD CORPORATION
All Rights Reserved   Used by Permission

I WILL KEEP MY EYES ON YOU

Refrain:
I will keep my eyes on You, I will be strong in Your power.
No matter what the cost, I will follow where You lead me.
In Your mighty strength I will stand by the power of Your hand,
I will keep my eyes on You.

Lord, I will follow, follow where You lead.
And as I obey You, You'll supply my every need.
Help me to live each day by faith, and not by sight,
Guided by Your Spirit's light.

Bridge:
In my weakness, You are strong.
All praise and glory to You belong.
In Your strength, I can sing the victor's song.

Words and Music by CINDY BERRY
© 1997 HAL LEONARD CORPORATION
This Arrangement © 2009 HAL LEONARD CORPORATION
All Rights Reserved   Used by Permission

NEW EVERY MORNING

Blessed Father, holy God, evermore the same,
Humbly now I come to You, trusting Your holy name.
You are my Rock, my fortress strong, giver of all good things.
When I think of your love and faithfulness, how can I help but sing?

Refrain:
New every morning,
New every morning are Your love and compassion, O Lord.
In Your mercy You have given me an anchor for my soul.
You saved and redeemed me, cleansed and made me whole.
New every morning, as day is dawning,
Your blessed hope and mercy I see.
Firm and secure, steadfast and sure,
Great is Your faithfulness to me.

Bridge:
Though trials come, and fears assail me,
Though winds of doubt may blow,
Safe in Your arms, sheltered from harm,
I can rejoice for this I know, that...

New every morning,
New every morning are Your love and compassion, O Lord.
In Your mercy You have given me an anchor for my soul.
You saved and redeemed me, cleansed and made me whole.
New every morning, as day is dawning,
Your blessed hope and mercy I see.
Firm and secure, steadfast and sure,
Great is Your faithfulness to me.
Great is Your faithfulness to me,
New every morning.

Words and Music by CINDY BERRY
© 2006 ALFRED PUBLISHING CO., INC.
This Arrangement © 2009 ALFRED PUBLISHING CO., INC.
All Rights Reserved

BY THE GENTLE WATERS

By the gentle waters, You will safely lead me,
In green pastures feed me, knowing what is best.
Though I often stray, wander far away,
I can hear You say, "Come to Me and rest."

Though the path be rough and rugged,
Though the trail be dark and steep,
Still the gentle Shepherd
Watches o'er His sheep.

There's no need to fear when the Shepherd's near.
When Your voice I hear, I find comfort sure.
Free from all alarm, sheltered from all harm,
Safely in Your arms, I can rest secure.

Bridge:
With the flock abiding, all my needs supplying,
Comforting and guiding, leading all the way, all the way.

Jesus, loving Shepherd, You'll forsake me never.
In Your flock forever, I am not alone.
Though the darkness hide me, You are close beside me.
Gentle Shepherd, guide me 'til I'm safely home,
'Til I'm safely home, safely home.

ALMIGHTY, UNCHANGEABLE GOD

Who spread out the clouds before Him?
Who fashioned the earth with His hands?
Who created the starry host, and formed the earth at His command?
Who scatters lightning before Him,
Commands the rain and snow to fall?
Who makes the nations tremble?
Who is Lord over all?

Refrain:
He is almighty, unchangeable God,
King of kings, Lord of lords, robed in majesty.
He rules and reigns for all eternity,
Almighty, unchangeable God.

He is like the light of sunrise,
Like the brightness after the rain,
Seated on His heavenly throne above.
His glory fills the heavens;
He is exalted over all.
Yet He loves me with an everlasting love.

YOURS IS THE KINGDOM

All praise I give to You alone, Father and Creator,
Alpha and Omega, Redeemer and Sustainer.
Holy Lamb of God, blessed Prince of Peace,
I will never cease to praise You.

Refrain:
For Yours is the kingdom, Yours is the power,
And the glory forever, forevermore.

I could never comprehend the grace You've freely given.
Wondrous is Your love for me, higher than the heavens.
As I abide in You, as You live through me,
May others see Your glory.

Bridge:
As I bow before You, I would give You praise.
I would serve You only, and walk in Your ways.

For Yours is the kingdom, Yours is the power,
And the glory forever, forevermore,
Forevermore, amen.

A STRONG TOWER

Let the name of the Lord be praised!
Let the name of the Lord be praised!
Great and mighty are His ways.
We will serve Him all our days.
Blessed be the name of the Lord.

Refrain:
The name of the Lord is a strong Tower,
A Tower in which we can hide.
Our Redeemer and Savior will always be our Shield and Guide.
As we trust in His name, we will find salvation;
He is our strength and our song.
To Him all praise and glory evermore belong.

Bridge:
One day every knee in heaven and earth will bow,
And every tongue will proclaim
That Jesus Christ is King of kings and Lord of lords.
He is the name that is above all names, above all names.

Let the name of the Lord be praised!
Let the name of the Lord be praised!
Great and mighty are His ways.
We will serve Him all our days.
Blessed be the great and matchless name of the Lord, of the Lord!

JOY OVERFLOWING

When I consider the heavens above,
The moon and the stars that Thou hast ordained,
When I consider Thy merciful love,
How can I help but sing?

Refrain:
And my praise will be ever to Thee,
Ever to Thee, O Lord,
The Great I Am, redeemer of man,
And giver of joy overflowing.

Mountains and hills burst forth into song.
The trees clap their hands; the heavens rejoice.
All creation sings for joy,
And I must add my voice.

Bridge:
Great King Eternal,
Lord of hosts, Prince of Peace, Ancient of days,
Thou art worthy,
Worthy of glory, majesty and praise.

And my praise will be ever to Thee,
Ever to Thee, O Lord,
The Great I Am, redeemer of man,
And giver of joy overflowing,
Giver of life, giver of love,
Giver of joy overflowing.

Words and Music by CINDY BERRY
© 1994 GLORYSOUND, A Division of SHAWNEE PRESS, INC.
This Arrangement © 2009 GLORYSOUND,
A Division of SHAWNEE PRESS, INC.
All Rights Reserved including Public Performance
Used by Permission